To: Mr. Welton, Junior,

face life and determination!

[signature]

Good luck with College!

Dec/3/06

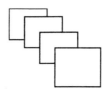

FACE LIFE SQUARELY

Face Life Squarely

ISBN: 0-9745227-1-6

Artistic Works and Designer: Dr. Kenwyn Williams
Editors: Michelle Fearon, Suzette Henry, Dr. Isaac Newton
The Author can be reached via e-mail: isanew@hotmail.com

FACE LIFE SQUARELY

Dr. Isaac James Newton

HEM Enterprises Ltd.
Trinidad West Indies.

iii

Contents

Dedication

- I honor my loving mother, Mrs. Josephine Newton, whose face serves as a library of wisdom and carries a rare brand of love. I dedicate the book to her husband, my dad, Mr. Moses Newton, whose face had the character of sacrificial and steady care without the cosmetics of parenting.

- To my brothers and sisters who shared their faces with me not merely by biological decree but in supportive sibling relationship. They were always spiritually, emotionally and psychologically present, even in their physical absence. We know one another's faces through and through.

- To my nieces and nephews whose curious, reassuring and amazing faces have brought me singing joy and sighing relief. You have made me proud to fulfill my assigned status and familial role as your uncle.

Acknowledgements

I owe the idea for the book to my initial infrequent glances at unfamiliar and familiar faces in my travel episodes around the world. Imperceptibly, I switched from glancing to observing and now to envisioning the life stories encapsulated in facial expressions.

I have learnt the difference between a face and a person without becoming addicted to the anticipated discovery that is realized in greeting and meeting different peoples and learning new lessons about life, constantly.

I have yet to imagine how I will respond to a faceless person but I know that even when there was a language barrier between strangers and myself, our communication mode was reduced to the universal language of our faces. And for this I thank them.

I appreciate the facial depictions that Dr. Kenwyn Williams created and as a result has made the book come to life. He is my friend and he knows it. To all my other friends who have given me access to their facial expressions, I do not want to commit the cardinal sin of naming some of you at the unforgivable expense of leaving others out. My gratitude belongs to you. Seth, Sue, Jon oh, Miche, Stan Ann, Fati and Di, your faces have been comforting in and out of seasons and for this, I am very thankful.

To HEM Enterprises Ltd. for getting the book done on time, thanks much!

To the Author and Finisher of my faith, The Almighty, all honor and glory belongs to you.

I.J.N.
New Jersey, USA
August 5, 2003

FACE LIFE SQUARELY

Preface

Faces are nature's unique stamps of approval forecasting the vanishing wonderment, obscure attractions, infinite curiosity, unriddled misgivings and mischievous charisma favored by the gestures of living.

They confirm the DNA of our identities, shoving out the self in us that protrudes itself through us. By depicting configurations of our emotions that are deposited through tickling the inner sanctuaries of our spirits, faces market our feelings, sell our reactions and label our interactions.

Examine a face carefully and you will find expressions capturing engraved aspirations, soaking-wet exhaustion, eye-squeezing hurts, and heart-beating celebrations compressed into exhilarating laughter. Without our faces, birth-cries caused by our out of womb environmental contact, and the frozen state of lifelessness produced by death, would leave no record for our memory to capture.

The paradoxes of being and becoming propelling us to live between constraint and freedom, demand that we should face life squarely with practical-minded serenity, smiling thirst, blood-clotting defiance, humored loss of composure, unmatched fortitude and undisguised faith.

Face life squarely is a story about the miraculous in our facial expressions and our facial expressions in the marvelous. How we handle this realization is indeed, the real story about our souls, our sanity, and our solace.

Dr. Isaac Newton

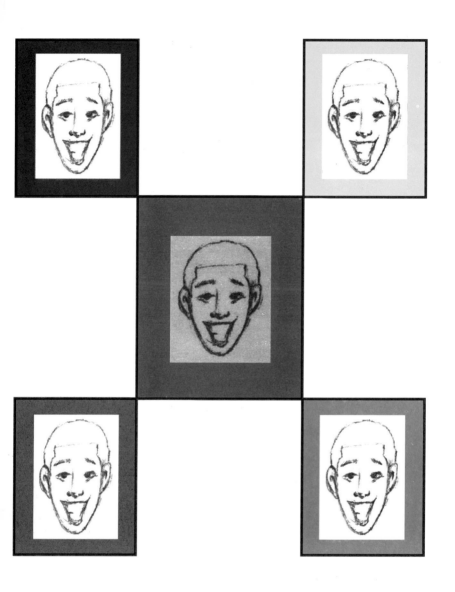

Dr. Isaac Newton

Chapter One
With A Smile

Face Life Squarely:

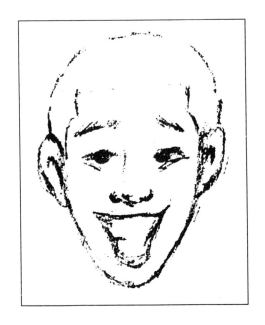

With a Smile that evokes the never to be defeated internal emotions and radiates the happiness and self-confidence you harbor!

1

Principle 1

I will concentrate on the bright side of life, judging myself by the sincere actions of my heart, without denying the ugliness of living.

Chapter Two
With A Laugh

Face Life Squarely:

With a Laugh that expresses the beauty and fun-filled vitality of your individuality!

Principle 2

I will remain alert to the monotony and resist the dullness of waking up every morning to my past wounds. A jovial spirit will be my guiding light.

Chapter Three
With A Wink

Face Life Squarely:

With a Wink that celebrates the un-noticed wonder-packed little things about your surrounding!

Principle 3

I will not take for granted
the many awesome
lessons that life shows
me in the tiny swing
and small momentum of
my daily environment.
Instead, I will let them
inspire me to value the
depth of living with the
mystery of being alive.

Chapter Four
With A Frown

Face Life Squarely:

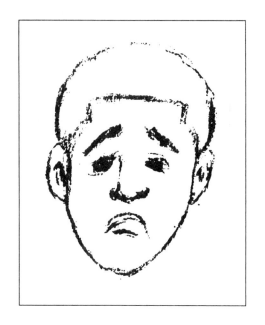

With a Frown that terminates acts or attitudes of injustice in whatever forms they come!

Principle 4

I am resolved to be
faithful to the dictates of
my own dignity and
integrity so that I do not
violate the universal values
I hold to be sacred.

Chapter Five
With Tears

Face Life Squarely:

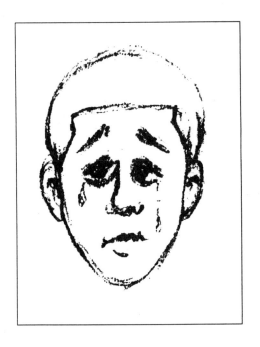

With Tears that absorb and wash away all of your hurts until healing arrives in its place!

Principle 5

I am committed to releasing the power of fresh insights, practical resources and newness of being that emerge out of life's heartbreaking pains.

Chapter Six
With A Stare

Face Life Squarely:

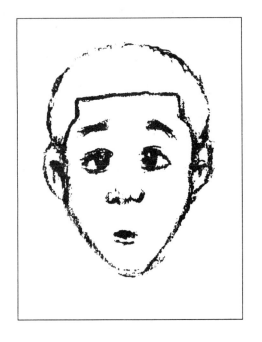

With a Stare that focuses your passions in the pursuit of your goals!

Principle 6

I am determined to convert every moment of discouragement and activity of failure, into formulating the crucial elements needed for celebrating victory and experiencing triumph.

Chapter Seven
With A Kiss

Face Life Squarely:

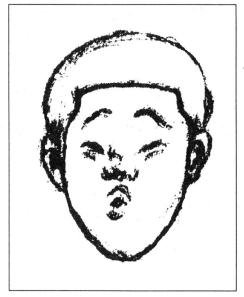

With a Kiss that affirms your triplet state of loving existence: Love for The Divine, love for The Divine in you and Love for The Divine in others!

Principle 7

I pledge my allegiance to the redemptive power of love that honors my spiritual obligation to the Divine, empowers me to become a more compassionate person, and fosters a healthy sense of neighborliness accommodating my dedication to the common good.

Chapter Eight

With A Sneeze

Face Life Squarely:

With a Sneeze that rids your
system of destructive
behavioral patterns and
negative energies!

Principle 8

I am decisive about
cleansing myself of all
emotional, experiential and
psychological sickness that
clutters my life space.

Chapter Nine
With A Smirk

Face Life Squarely:

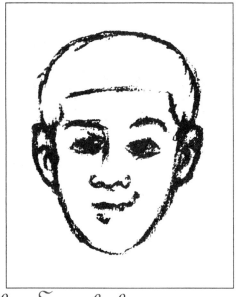

With a Smirk that demonstrates your refusal to cooperate with tendencies that fixate you to your have been's, cripples your could be's and burns up your now's!

Principle 9

Under NO circumstances will I ever allow myself to avoid the invigorating freshness of every breathing moment. My indomitable spirit will force me to live vibrantly and passionately at all times, soaring ahead, seeing afar, stretching above and reaching beyond every perceived limitation.

Chapter Ten
With A Grin

Face Life Squarely:

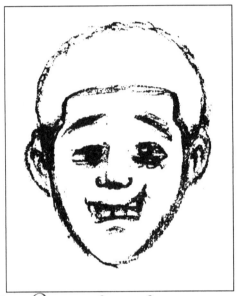

With a Grin that showcases your confidence to withstand and tenacity to endure the devastating experiences that muddy your pathway!

Principle 10

I will not be deterred
by any disaster,
disillusionment and demonic
influences that assail me.
From this day, I will not
trade honesty, cheapen
justice, or boycott grace.

Chapter Eleven
With Anger

Face Life Squarely:

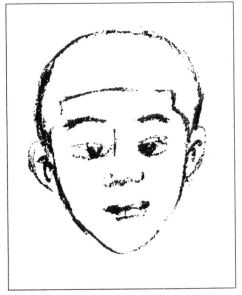

With Anger that positively denounces actions, attitudes, behaviors, conversations and non-verbal subtleties designed to ruin your life!

Principle 11

I stand against being remote-controlled by the destructive effects of anger but will use it as a powerful life-force that enlivens, matures, and enlightens my vision of self-development. Tough calmness and fierce peace will govern my orientation in relating to others.

Chapter Twelve
With A Blush

Face Life Squarely:

With a Blush that captures the
soft/shy side of being your
unique self!

Principle 12

I am determined to
become a more sensitive,
humble and affectionate
person regardless of the
mean-spirited actions of
others, and my own
ominous deficiencies.